VINTAGE CAR
WRECKS

Motoring Mishaps
1950-1979

Rusty Herlocher

Published by

An F&W Publications Company

700 East State Street • Iola, WI 54990-0001
715-445-2214 • 888-457-2873
www.krause.com

Please call or write for our free catalog of publications.
Our toll-free number to place an order or obtain a free catalog is (800) 258-0929
or please use our regular business telephone (715) 445-2214.

Library of Congress Catalog Number: 2002113157
ISBN: 0-87349-458-X

Printed in the United States of America

Acknowledgments

I would like to thank and gratefully acknowledge the generosity of those who supplied photographs, helping to make this book possible. A special thanks to John J. Yahner and Robert O. Rolley, Jr. for their kind indulgence and professional assistance. Thanks to John "Jack" Frey, Rick Noll, *The Lock Haven Express*, *The Williamsport Sun Gazett*, Stiely's Garage, Susan Bacchieri and the guys at Hoyer's Photo Supply, and my in-laws, Pat and Bill Tyson, for cleaning up my literary blunders.

Most importantly, thank you to the official Herlocher Pit Crew Chief, my beautiful wife and soul mate, Dawn.

Introduction

It seems like only yesterday that I anxiously awaited the arrival of the new models at the local Chevy dealer. He carefully papered the windows closed, whetting the appetites of all the car nuts in town. We would wait breathlessly for the uncovering, that magical moment when the sun would reflect and glisten off the treasure trove of bright shiny chrome that oozed from and onto every conceivable panel, nook and cranny. I swear that a tear came to my eye the first time I saw the new 1960 Chevy Impala. For me, nothing, except the birth of my children, can match the thrill of witnessing the arrival of the new models. It is fruitless to try to explain this feeling to someone whose calendar year does not coincide with the new car release.

As a youth I would read every word of every brochure that I could get my hands on. I walked to the Pontiac dealership, (far beyond where I was permitted to go and absolutely forbidden by my mother) to pick one (that's all the owner would allow) brochure of each model. I had a definite opinion of each style and made no attempt to curb my enthusiasm or dissatisfaction.

I remember the smell, I tell you I can still remember the smell that hovered in the air when opening the door of a new '58 Continental Mark III. The supple Scottish leather is the heady stuff that dreams are made of.

There are times and events in ones life that are etched forever. You know what you were doing when President Kennedy was assassinated. You know where you were when you heard that Elvis died, and you remember the first time you saw a Ford Mustang.

Those days are long gone in all but our memories. Now the new models come out with no fan fair. Next year's models are released in the middle of the summer. I can't remember the last time I saw a flashing bust of chrome. Maybe my children will fondly remember the new 2000 Buick or Honda, but I doubt it.

There was nothing ho-hum about Chryslers mean and lean wedge head V-8, or Dodge and Plymouth's 426 Hemi, not to mention the wild Pontiac 421 that assaulted the streets during the '60s. Can you imagine anyone today paying tribute to an engine like the Beach Boys did with the Chevy 409? It just seems the thrill is gone. Today's lackluster cars possess neither character nor pizzazz. The look-alike styling and performance prove the lack of innovation in design. There is no rumble from a fine-tuned exhaust system (the one exception is the 2001 Mustang GT Cobra, a sweet sound that can bring a baby boomer to his knees). In fact, most cars remind me of an egg that just rolls down the street, oval, smooth and quiet with not a hint of class or sass.

No matter your political opinion of DeLorean, there just doesn't seem to be anyone with his kind of flare and blatant ingenuity. His '64 GTO was truly a thing of beauty and ignited the muscle car fires. He showed plenty of courage by going against GM's edict forbidding anything larger than a 330-cubic inch engine in an intermediate body by offering his GTO package. The earth trembled, and goose bumps went up your spine just standing next to a rumbling Hurst.

Soccer moms and pony drivers everywhere owe a debt to Lee Iacocca's imagination and intuition. Arguably two of the most influential vehicles of all times, the hot little Mustang that opened a whole new territory of performance, and the mini-van, were a result of his creative genius.

Only an industry unencumbered by today's regulations could pursue new frontiers of high performance of the '50s and '60s. The style of the proud fins of a Chrysler. A Mustang hunched down and ready to roar at a full gallop. The incredible lines of the '56 T-Bird with porthole windows and a continental tire out back. The brassy, loud Yenko Camaro that did the quarter mile in 11.94 seconds at 114.5 mph. The list goes on

By the '70s the sun was beginning to set on the full-blown, tire-smoking, road-ripping muscle cars. Buick and Oldsmobile skunked the competition with the Grand Sport and the 4-4-2 — road rockets that were disguised as luxury cars. Even American Motors got into the act with a potent little surprise called the AMX. But insurance rates, safety concerns, fuel prices, emissions laws and government regulations brought it all to a screeching halt by the mid '70s.

You probably get the picture; I'm a hard-core roadman. There isn't a car I don't like.

A 1967 Chevrolet Bel-Air was a total loss after this accident

It was this love of the automobile that led to the strange hobby of collecting photographs of vehicle accidents. I love cars. I love to look at cars. I love to drive cars. My favorite past time was, and is, driving to car lots to check out the merchandise. I make my living and support my wife of 30 years and our 3 children selling cars. The shelves of my library are full of car books. I have collected car literature and sales albums for years. My sport of choice is car racing, which leads to an assortment of photographs.

During my youth there was very little information available about car races. I would trek to every dirt track I could. I remember watching Jimmy Spencer's father race. Now if you want to talk about excitement, you should have seen his old man run the course.

I would cut school and hitch a ride to Watkins Glen and stand breathless as the likes of Sterling Moss, Phil Hill and Briggs Cunningham sped by. But any news coverage concerning the big races was limited to a few lines in the newspaper. Any photo that was published had to be sensational, so of course it was the wrecks that received print space.

I started collecting photos of car wrecks in 1953, mainly due to my interest in auto racing. I still have the photograph that sparked my interest in accidents and subsequently automobile safety. A New York paper ran a story of a man that, while traveling at a high rate of speed, lost control of his car. It plunged through a fence and crashed into a telephone pole. The force was so terrific that the body of the victim was catapulted through the vehicle's windshield straight up into the telephone wires. The photo showed the demolished 1948 Chevy sitting against the pole and the victim's body dangling from the wires. The message of the story and photograph was the dangers of drinking and driving. I don't think I ever gave the car keys to one of the kids on a Friday night that I didn't think of that photograph.

Since that day in 1953 much has been done to improve the safety of cars. Through the efforts of manufacturers, often the results of activists and regulations, cars have evolved and improved with each new model.

Many parts of a car that we take for granted were originally "add-ons" that eventually were given "standard status." We may not think of a windshield, headlights, doors, bumpers, steel frames, flashing turn signals, padded dashes, rear view mirrors, speedometers, horns, windshield wipers, defrosters, shatterproof glass, shock absorbers, four-wheel brakes and instrument gauges as safety equipment, but they are.

Of course, no amount of innovations or regulations can compensate for a lack of safe driving. It is the responsibility of each person, when they sit behind the wheel to consciously decide to be a safe and courtesy driver. Unfortunately many drivers overestimate their ability and underestimate conditions. Statistics prove that 99 out of every 100 people will be involved in an automobile accident at some point in their lives.

Driving while under the influence of alcohol and other drugs is a leading cause of accidents and deaths each year. The latest government totals claim that close to 40 percent of the nearly 50,000 automobile accident fatalities a year are alcohol related. This is a problem that no mechanical improvement or safety feature can rectify.

To listen to some of the politicians talk it would seem as though half of the corporate world is out to kill us. The tobacco industry and the automobile industry top the list of ultimate mercenaries. Actually automobile manufactures would love to be able to say, "In our cars you will never have another accident and if you do you will not be hurt". Of course this is impossible, but they can and do achieve improvements each year.

The following examples of accidents in this book are loosely grouped chronologically, beginning with a few in the 1940s and running through the 1970s. Volkswagens are featured at the end, with no attempt to offer their production year.

This book is not an attempt to glorify these accidents in any way, or profit from the misfortune of the participants. In some cases, the accidents are almost humorous. Sadly, many were tragic. Hopefully, the images that follow serve simply as a photographic record and harsh reminder of the consequences of unsafe, or unlucky, driving.

The trauma this 1960 Buick and its driver suffered from a horrendous accident is painfully obvious.

1950s and Before

The moves of the Brooklyn Dodgers and the New York Giants to California notwithstanding, the 1950s proved to be a post-war feel-good decade. Rampant consumerism and a decade-long speeding spree exemplified the credo of instant gratification. There were pink Cadillacs and 15-cent McDonald's hamburgers. The unprecedented prosperity rolled this affluent society effortlessly along on Firestone whitewalls. The American automobile of the 1950s may have been all grinning chrome tooth grills and Marilyn Monroe silhouette curves, but it fueled a new industrial prosperity that made motor-driven America the envy of the world.

A lot was going on in this vibrant country of ours. Gas stations were staffed with several bright-eyed, scrubbed-faced attendants that were eager to wash your windows, check your tires and oil, fill your tank, present you with a free gift and even give you S & H Green Stamps. Tail fins grew to unbridled proportions — Cadillac's soared up, Chevy's reached out and Buick called theirs "delta

Photo courtesy of Jack Frey

A 1948 Chrysler Windsor two-door convertible six-cylinder and a 1955 Hudson Custom complete with Continental Kit had an unhappy union. A student driving the Chrysler slammed into the car owned by the superintendent of the school. The student explained to police that he mistakenly stepped on the gas pedal instead of the brake, went through the stop sign, and hit the superintendent's car.

wings." President Eisenhower proposed a new interstate highway system. The Federal Highway Act was passed. Marlon Brando inspired millions of young men to sport "ducktail" haircuts and deliver responses casually mumbled. James Dean died in a car crash. Hugh Hefner launched *Playboy* magazine. The first successful open-heart surgery was performed. And in Memphis a young man laid out $4 to cut a record for his mother's birthday and signed the card: "Love, Elvis."

The National Production Authority announced cutbacks as the Korean War intensified, the government ordered a price ceiling, and regulation "W" limited credit terms to 15 months with 1/3 down payment required. While we listened to American BandStand legislation was introduced to require seatbelts and a team of five legislators visited Detroit, hinting at the prospect of a safe car law. The American Automobile Association urged manufacturers to emphasize safety not speed, and

announced that crank case ventilation devices would be installed on all vehicles in California. Before long emissions and safety issues would influence the way we felt about our cars and the manufacturers that built them.

Of the 1 million vehicles tested in 1954 by the state-sponsored "check your car program," one quarter flunked the safety test. One more brick was laid in the foundation of government regulation. Congressional hearings produced the "Automobile Information Disclosure Act" mandating window stickers displayed in every new car with serial number and suggested retail price.

A decade that began with an added cost for back-up lights ended with such safety improvements as the padded roof, quad headlamps, one-piece windshield, step-down steel frame, hill-holder transmissions, turn signals and back-up lights, tubeless tires, and door locks.

This 1948 Plymouth Deluxe coupe suffered damage when rammed and shoved about 20 feet by a tractor-trailer truck at a busy city intersection. The truck driver reported that he could not stop when the traffic light changed because of brake failure.

A 1948 Plymouth Special Deluxe four-door sedan was parked along the street, minding its own business, when struck by a 1955 Chevrolet Bel Air four-door sedan as it rounded the corner. Note the optional sun visor added to the Plymouth.

This 1949 Studebaker Champion two-door and a 1955 Oldsmobile Super 88 four-door sedan were both badly damaged in a head-on collision that occurred at a busy "Y" in the road.

Photo courtesy of Jack Frey

Unfortunately for this 1949 Plymouth Deluxe, it crashed head-on into a tractor-trailer truck. The force of the impact crumpled the front end, shoved the motor back under the dashboard, and buckled the frame into a "V". In contrast to the wrecked car is the brand-new 1958 Ford Custom sedan police radio cruiser, which went into service just two days prior to the taking of this photograph.

A Plymouth Special Deluxe 6 sedan and an early 1950s Chevrolet panel truck cozy up in an accident that was more entertaining than damaging.

This 1949 Plymouth Deluxe coupe was towed into the garage to evaluate the damage suffered following a roll into a shallow ravine.

A 1949 Plymouth four-door had quite an adventure. The Plymouth, seen at top, was stolen from a used car lot, and while being chased by police at a high rate of speed the stolen car skidded out of control, sideswiped and damaged two parked cars; the 1956 Chrysler Windsor four-door sedan in the middle and a 1951 Ford Custom Victoria two-door hardtop at the bottom. A wire fence and a clothesline, seen in the top of the composite picture, ensnared the thief and hindered his escape.

This 1950 Ford Custom two-door coupe and a 1950 Chevrolet Styleline Deluxe coupe formed a most perfect union. The young man stopped to inspect the wreckage while trying to look "cool" and stay warm. Note the extra-cost sun visor and spotlight on the Ford.

A 1950 Mercury Monterey two-door coupe made a mess on the street that the fire department was forced to clean.

This 1950 Chevrolet was demolished when struck by a train. A police investigation and a coroner's inquest exonerated the railroad watchman of any responsibility or criminal negligence in this accident. All witnesses agreed that the car attempted to beat the train to the crossing.

This 1950 Buick Special Sedanet speeded past two cars before being forced from the road by an oncoming truck. The Buick crossed the highway diagonally before impaling itself on a bridge railing.

A 1950 Buick Special four-door sedan lands in a dandy position for a grease job. The police report states "no details" concerning this accident in which the grille so ensnarled the trunk of a tree that it came to rest in this position. The car apparently skidded its way up the inclining tree and received support from the open door on the driver's side.

This 1950 Oldsmobile 88 four-door sedan traveled several blocks the wrong way on a one-way street, cut across into a municipal parking lot, where a sleek, new 1959 Dodge Coronet four-door sedan with the special deluxe two-tone paint treatment was about to exit. The Olds skidded and hit a utility pole before hitting the Dodge in the side.

A 1950 Chevrolet Styleline Deluxe takes an offbeat parking spot. A few bricks were crushed, the windows were smashed, several toys were broken, a parking meter post was snapped off, and the Chevy received moderate damage. The driver told police she was trying to pull into a parking space when the brakes failed and the car jumped the curb. Notice the Dinky Toys, Daisy air guns, Whimsies dolls, and other popular toy collectibles scattered about the storefront.

A 16-year-old boy attained his driver's license just hours before this misadventure. The 1950 Plymouth Deluxe four-door was badly damaged because the driver lacked the experience to right the car after it went off the road at a deceptively wicked curve.

This 1950 Buick Super four-door sedan must have taken aim at the 1957 Dodge Coronet four-door sedan to have so accurately struck the grille dead center. The accident report makes no mention of the overturned Chevrolet delivery van in the background.

A new car delivered quite a jolt to this 1950 Chevrolet Styleline Special coupe. The 1958 Rambler American two-door coupe, still wearing a temporary license plate, pulled from a church parking lot and right into the side of the passing Chevy.

Leaving the road for a "close encounter" with a guardrail was this 1951 Ford Custom Club coupe with an add-on hood emblem. The driver was to be married the next day. This was Ford's first year for an automatic transmission, called Ford-o-matic.

A 1951 Ford Custom Club coupe slammed into a pole, causing the passenger to be thrown against the windshield. Note the "V" on the fender signifying a 239-cid V-8 engine.

A 1951 Chevrolet Styleline Deluxe two-door was hit on the left side by a 1956 Pontiac Catalina two-door hardtop. A 1956 Pontiac outperformed all V-8s in the Mobilgas Economy Run.

This 1951 Chevrolet Styleline Special two-door sedan six-cylinder left the road going airborne and made a precarious landing just short of the railroad track.

1951 Ford Custom Fordor four-door sedan took it on the chin. The driver pulled to the side of the road to watch a flock of wild turkeys in a meadow, but parked too close to the edge and the Ford simply fell onto its side and landed on a large rock.

The driver of this 1951 Oldsmobile 88 two-door coupe survived the crash, but drowned shortly after. Failing to make a curve, the car overturned into a ditch. It is believed that the driver was trapped in the car for several hours before a passing motorist discovered the accident. After receiving reassurance that help would be forthcoming, the driver crawled from the wreck into the water-filled ditch and drowned.

After an unsuccessful attempt to pass another vehicle, the driver of this 1951 Plymouth Concord Savoy two-door Suburban ended up in a wheat field. The Concord Savoy replaced the Special Deluxe Suburban for 1951 and became Plymouth's fanciest station wagon-type vehicle, since the "woodie" option was dropped from the P-23 series.

A 1951 Chevrolet Styleline Deluxe four-door sedan, minus fender skirts, crashed head-on with a 1953 Plymouth Cambridge Suburban station wagon.

1951 Chrysler Saratoga four-door sedan is being towed from a three-way train crossing where it was struck by a Pennsylvania Railroad passenger train. The driver was thrown from the car upon impact and suffered only slight abrasions. The Chrysler was not as fortunate. Note the tire chains on the rear wheel added for traction on winter roads.

This 1951 Pontiac Chieftain two-door, a once proud automobile, has been reduced to this mass of metal after being subjected to abuse. Excessive speed caused the driver to lose control rounding a curve and the car rolled up an embankment, hit a tree, upended, and slid down the road some 189 feet before being halted by the guard wire.

A 1951 Ford Custom two-door sedan flaunting an added eagle-wing emblem, 1955 hubcaps, and a "Civil Defense" plate on the front bumper waits patiently in the cold for repairs.

A 1951 Chevrolet Styleline Deluxe two-door sedan nudged a 1954 Ford Customline with wild fender skirts, dual exhaust, custom taillights and wide whitewall tires. The Ford then bumped into a 1953 Ford two-door. The commotion disrupted this otherwise idealistic tree lined, brick neighborhood. Was life ever so simple and innocent.

When this 1951 Studebaker Champion two-door happened upon a patch of icy road, it met with a porch foundation and spun around to show off its new profile.

This 1952 Chevrolet Styleline Deluxe four-door sedan left the road and rolled over into a field. Note the distinctive swan hood ornament.

A 1952 Cadillac Series 62 four-door sedan donated its rear taillight to a 1954 Plymouth Belvedere four-door sedan. 1952 was Cadillac's Golden Anniversary year and special trim features were added to each series. For Series 62s, the deck emblem was the Cadillac crest over a golden "V."

Photo courtesy of Jack Frey

A car hidden from view in this photo dealt a deathblow to this 1952 Cadillac Hearse. The 1954 Ford driver drove onto the sidewalk to avoid injury. The carcass of the doomed hearse is being towed.

This unfortunate 1952 Willys Aero-Lark coupe was the sole participant in this one-car accident, which occurred when the driver lost control, struck a sign, and overturned late one Saturday night. Styled by designer Phil Wright and engineered by Clyde Paton, the Aero Lark was the base trim level and used the 161-cid/75-hp inline six-cylinder engine.

A 1952 Chevrolet Styleline Deluxe four-door sedan (top) is inspected after being pulled from the front portch that it destroyed just hours before. If you think the car looks wretched, just take a look at the devastated remains of the portch. (below)

Photo courtesy of Jack Frey

A 1952 Ford Customline two-door with special add-on molding and paint passed the 1957 Chevrolet Two-Ten two-door hardtop before it collided with a third car that approached from the opposite direction. The Chevrolet then drove into the ditch to avoid another car that stopped suddenly when a truck just ahead of it hit and killed a deer right in front of the Rod and Gun Club. Six people were taken to the hospital as a result of this mess, but all were quickly released with only minor cuts and bruises.

Photo courtesy of Jack Frey

A young veteran returning home in his 1952 Ford Customline two-door sedan skidded and crashed sideways into the oncoming 1958 Chevrolet Biscayne four-door sedan. Thanks to the State Trooper's flashlight, we are able to get a glimpse of the damage done to the inside of the Chevy. Note the bent steering wheel and broken windshield—both injury inflicting damages that would have been diminished with seat belts and air bags.

Photo courtesy of The Williamsport Sun-Gazette

This 1952 Lincoln Capri four-door sedan provided a bumpy, scary ride for two young lovers the night before being towed to this salvage yard. The couple was parked at a favorite spot when the young lady heard a noise, became frightened, and convinced her friend it was time to leave. He mistakenly put the car in drive rather than reverse, stepped on the gas, and promptly plunged them over the 300-foot drop until a tree stopped their descent. Except for a few bruises and a difficult time explaining to their parents what they were doing at the notorious spot, the couple was unhurt.

Photo courtesy of The Williamsport Sun-Gazette

The corner of a brick building marked the end of the road for this 1952 Chevrolet Skyleliner Deluxe Sport. Note the WWPA sign in the back window. The Chevy belonged to a county employee charged with regulating the pollution level in the water supply.

This 1953 Chevrolet Two-Ten four-door sedan suffered damages when it swerved into the opposite lane to avoid a sudden landslide, then swerved back into the slide to avoid an oncoming truck. The 235-cid six-cylinder engine was standard on this model, but the sun visor was an added option.

A 1953 DeSoto Firedome V-8 sedan rounded a corner and struck a jackknifed tractor-trailer. It then traveled 40 feet from the point of impact, avoiding both the tree in the background and a group of children that were playing in the yard.

Photo courtesy of The Lock Haven Express

The 1953 Plymouth Cranbrook four-door sedan only came with an inline six-cylinder engine. The young driver of this car was fatally injured when Pennsylvania Railroad's "Buffalo Flyer" crashed into his vehicle while it was stalled on a crossing. The demolished car was pushed 37 feet before the train was able to stop. 1953 was Plymouth's 25th anniversary year and saw a 39 percent increase in sales. In September, the 8 millionth Plymouth rolled off the assembly line.

Photo courtesy of Jack Frey

This 1953 Plymouth Cranbrook Club Coupe was seriously marred when struck in the rear by a coal truck. Although the damage appears to be confined to the rear, the hit was hard enough to dislodge the front seat, which was attached to the frame by only four bolts, a condition the National Highway Traffic Safety Administration thankfully would never allow today.

This 1953 Nash Statesman Super four-door sedan was not the only thing saved by the guardrail cable. The driver, unfamiliar with the winding mountain road, failed to negotiate a curve, plunged through the guardrails, and took the cable with it. The taut cable wrapped around the car and stopped it from tumbling onto a house at the bottom of the ravine.

Prior to its taking a swim, this 1953 Buick Special four-door sedan was parked on a slight incline. It is believed the gear slipped allowing it to roll diagonally down the bank and out into the river. Buoyancy carried the car about 40 feet down stream before it sank to the bottom. The car was hauled out onto the bank by a cable passed through the windows. The young driver ran after the car and jumped into the water after it, but his efforts were fruitless!

A 1953 Ford Customline two-door sedan was unable to stop at an ice-covered intersection and slid into an unyielding post.

A 1953 Cadillac Series 62 four-door sedan is the object of much attention after an unfortunate mishap.

A 1953 Cadillac 62 Series two-door hardtop could not avoid hitting an early Chevrolet. More interesting than the events that lead to the accident were the estimated damages as stated on the accident report dated October of 1954: $75 for the Chevrolet and $400 for Cadillac!

The center of attention on this quiet street was this wrecked 1953 Chevrolet Two-Ten four-door sedan. 1953 was the first year that Chevrolet offered power steering as an option.

This 1953 Studebaker Commander V-8 four-door sedan hurdled the guide wire and dropped 8 feet to land upright on the Pennsylvania Railroad track. Friends following closely behind came to the rescue by lifting the car from the tracks before a train came.

A 1953 Packard Mayfair two-door hardtop stopped in for coffee. The house and the car seem to have both suffered equal damage. Only 5,150 Mayfairs were produced in 1953. The Mayfair had the same trim appointments as the Clipper Deluxe, but came with a more lush interior and a base price of $3,278.

In this 1950s fender-bender, a 1953 Plymouth Cranbrook four-door sedan nudged a 1959 Pontiac Bonneville convertible. Petroliana collectors today should note the gas station complete with signs and glass-domed gas pumps.

As it is towed away, this 1953 Dodge Coronet two-door coupe clearly illustrates that snow-covered, icy roads are always hazardous, but especially so when the roads are heavily engaged with obstacles such as utility poles, trees, pedestrians, and fire alarm boxes.

A freight car being loaded at a feed mill to the right of the photo released and drifted into the rear of this unsuspecting 1953 Ford Customline two-door coupe that had just crossed the train track. The force of impact pushed the coupe onto a rock pile.

A 1953 Chevrolet Deluxe Two-Ten couldn't help vandalizing this mailbox after it was hit in the front end.

A 1953 Ford Customline four-door sedan tested the waters along the road. Note the raccoon tail hanging from the antenna—can't be much more '50ish than that.

This 1953 Oldsmobile Super 88 two-door sedan still retains the waxed shine of a pampered vehicle, but suffered greatly from its run-in with a tree. One of Oldsmobile's biggest sellers for the year, some 36,824 Super 88 two-door sedans hit the highways and the occasional tree.

Silent but sturdy, this 1953 Ford Customline two-door sedan with V-8 engine bares the combat scars it received on the asphalt battlefield. Its windshield, front end, and spirit are cracked, dented, but not defeated, and will be restored to ride another day.

The entire front end of this 1954 Hudson Hornet four-door sedan was demolished when it hit a truck, left the road, and eliminated a light pole and wire. The students at the elementary school just down the lane were happy when the interrupted electricity necessitated an early dismissal.

When the driver of this 1954 Oldsmobile Super 88 four-door sedan overcompensated for the bank of a curve, the Olds left the road and hit a tree. This same driver had the very same story just a week before after hitting the very same tree at the exact same location. Practice does not always make perfect.

This photo captures a 1954 Studebaker Champion Custom two-door sedan that faced east after traveling west. The force of the impact tore the utility pole through the car and suspended the rear end several feet in the air.

This 1954 Chevrolet Two-Ten four-door sedan appears to be quite a mess. It is amazing how quickly a crowd can gather to survey the damage from an accident.

The 1954 Oldsmobile 98 four-door sedan seen here plunged through a ravine, burst through a billboard like a rock through a paper bag, just missed a utility pole, sped through a half-filled maze-like parking lot, and buried its nose into the side of a hotel. The driver happily walked away with no injuries.

An unfortunate 1954 Ford Customline two-door sedan V-8 was harpooned by a bridge railing when the driver tried to make a lane change. Not only did he misjudge the number of lanes on the bridge, he also disregarded the posted 15 mph speed limit.

Patiently awaiting the tow truck is a 1954 Ford Customline four-door sedan with a V-8 engine as its driver accepts a lecture from the reporting officer. Note the chrome side window shades.

After this 1955 Chevrolet Bel Air convertible failed to negotiate a curve, it sheared a pole in half, and eased its backside onto a porch. This was the first year that Chevrolet offered a V-8 engine.

A wrecked 1955 Ford Fairlane Crown Victoria coupe. Of the 33,165 Crown Victorias built in '55, many were equipped with the V-8 engine.

This 1955 Ford Fairlane Town sedan was equipped with a 272-cid V-8 engine. It left the road, plowed through a mailbox, and was finally stopped by a tree.

A 1955 Ford Customline Tudor sedan with a 272-cid V-8 Ford-O-Matic proved no match for this tree. Note the add-on fender skirts.

A Jeep wrecker hauls off the 1955 Chevrolet Two-Ten Del Ray coupe with six-cylinder in which four women were injured. A witness told police that apparently the car hit a patch of ice, skidded across the highway, struck several guardrails, then bounced back across the road and into an embankment.

A 1955 Dodge Coronet four-door sedan rammed into a 1951 Kaiser Special four-door sedan. The Dodge, after being hit from behind, pushed the parked Kaiser 75 feet along the street and over the curb. Note the Kaiser's "Sweetheart Dip" in the upper portion of the back window.

A 1955 Chevrolet Two-Ten Del Ray coupe competes for road space with a 1955 Cadillac Series 62 four-door sedan. The young driver of the Chevy watches as the officer checks the license of the gentleman driving the Cadillac. According to the report, the Chevy was traveling west when the Cadillac made a "wide" right turn out of the side street into the path of the oncoming car.

A 1955 Mercury Montclair four-door sedan crashed through a wire fence and into a flagpole at a leather tanning plant. The driver was unhurt, but the 17-year-old passenger was critically injured.

A 1955 Studebaker Commander four-door sedan sideswiped this ill-fated home that was already undergoing repairs due to damages received from another traffic accident the previous month. The Studebaker suffered extensive damage when the driver lost control on a treacherous curve, hit the home, crashed into a utility pole, and finally came to rest against a porch.

This 1957 Ford Fairlane two-door sedan skidded more than 445 feet along the road's shoulder before it crashed into this dwelling. The 72-year-old resident, sleeping in the room directly above the broken window, was thrown from her bed by the impact.

This 1955 Buick Roadmaster two-door hardtop left the highway and drove into a house. The porch roof, partially resting on the car, collapsed to the ground after the vehicle was removed. The sharp lines and abundance of chrome help explain Buick's advancement to the number three spot in production during 1955.

This 1955 Chevrolet Bel Air convertible was demolished and two were seriously injured in an early morning crash that happened directly across the street from a city hospital. Shattered glass from the Chevy's windows was embedded in the tree trunk. Note the factory wire wheel covers.

An unfortunate 1955 Packard Clipper four-door sedan was unable to avoid an unmanned car that rolled down the hill. The runaway car was parked along a steep hill when it suddenly broke loose and cantered toward the unsuspecting Clipper, crushing the left front fender.

The impact of this 1955 Chevrolet 150 four-door sedan six-cylinder with a telephone pole was responsible for a communication disruption that spanned three communities for more than four hours. The officers inspect the damages received from the unfortunate run-in and note that both headlights popped out of their respective fenders, and the hood ornament is nowhere to be found.

Here's something you don't see every day—a 1955 Ford Fairlane Town four-door sedan involved in a head-on collision with a washing machine. The Maytag was a total washout, while the Ford, although agitated, was only slightly damaged.

A 1955 Oldsmobile Super 88 four-door sedan went through a red light and thrashed an unsuspecting 1951 Chevrolet Styleline Special.

This 1955 Buick Roadmaster was a battered but well-built automobile. This particular model was at least a quarter-ton heavier than other Buick models that year.

The rain adds insult to the injuries sustained by this 1955 Buick Special two-door sedan.

A 1956 Nash Rambler Custom Cross Country station wagon "t-boned" a 1951 Cadillac 62 Series four-door causing it to come to rest with a fire hydrant lodged beneath its right rear fender. Power steering was a new option for Nash in 1956 and might have come in handy here.

A 1956 Chevrolet Two-ten four-door sedan with a six-cylinder engine suffered fatal damage from a head-on collision with a heavy-duty truck. The police accident report listed "excessive speed" as the cause.

The interior of this Chevy two-ten (the same car shown on the bottom of previous page) reveals the complete devastation that resulted from this wreck.

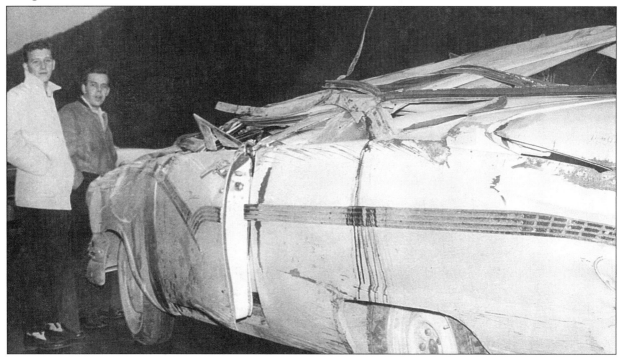

Two young men riding in a 1956 Ford Fairlane Victoria two-door hardtop rolled the car over and skidded into an embankment to avoid hitting a deer along a mountain road one Saturday night. Strange as it may seem, earlier that same day in exactly the same location another motorist swerved to avoid a deer and rolled his car over twice. In both cases, the cars were heavily damaged and the deer were not hurt.

The driver of this 1956 Ford Country four-door station wagon chose a poor spot to go wandering off the road. The impact was harsh enough to cause the passenger to hit her head on the windshield. Ford offered seat belts for the first time in 1956.

The 1956 Chevrolet 150 two-door sedan is inspected by the driver of the 1956 Buick Riviera two-door hardtop. The woman explains to the police officer that her dog ran out of the house and into the street, causing chaos. Apparently, the Buick swerved to avoid the puppy and hit the Chevy, which spun around. Then the Buick fishtailed, causing damage to the rear of the 1948 Oldsmobile in the background. The dog was unhurt.

This 1956 Ford Customline two-door with 173-hp 272-cid V-8 was completely demolished. There doesn't seem to be anything unusual about this particular stretch of highway that claimed the life of the Ford driver, but it has been the scene of several fatalities. This night, high speed was no doubt responsible for the Ford's intrusion into the opposite lane and slamming into the truck (seen in the background by the broken utility pole). Note the rear of the Packard ambulance at far left of photo.

This 1956 Buick Special two-door hardtop was smashed beyond repair when it was sideswiped by a gas field trailer truck.

When this 1956 Chevrolet Two-Ten Sports Sedan four-door hardtop was forced from the highway by an unidentified car, the young couple inside plummeted down the steep, rocky mountain. A well-placed tree stopped the tumbling car just short of the raging river.

The 1956 Ford Thunderbird convertible came with a 292-cid V-8 as standard, but 90 percent of the 15,631 produced carried the optional 312-cid V-8 engine. It is difficult for any Thunderbird enthusiast to look at a Bird in this condition, and making it worse is the fact that the car was only one day old. The driver bought the car that morning, then raced down the highway late that night, lost control, and flew into a heavily wooded area, buckling and twisting the rear end almost beyond recognition. Note the hardtop lying in the back seat.

While attempting to pass another car, this 1956 Ford Custom Ranch two-door station wagon left the road, hit a rock, and rolled over several times.

This 1956 Plymouth Savoy four-door sedan was driven by a schoolteacher who failed basic driving lessons. According to the police report, the car went off the road and hit a telephone pole after illegally attempting to pass a tractor-trailer then cutting back into its lane. The driver was thrown from the nearly demolished car before the severed pole landed atop it. Note the other autos in this field: a 1950 Nash and 1930s Ford Model A.

A 1956 Chevrolet Two-Ten four-door sedan with a 265-cid V-8 engine was slightly rearranged when hit from the side.

A 1956 Chevrolet Bel Air four-door hardtop was demolished after being stolen by a 15-year-old boy and his girlfriend. They fled from the state police at speeds topping 100 mph. Unable to control the vehicle, the teens left the highway, snapped off a guardrail post, hit a freshly-graded earth fill, and flipped into the front yard of the Pennsylvania State Police barracks. The car came within six inches of the building near a room where a trooper was sleeping. The teens were thrown clear of the vehicle and escaped serious injury.

This 1956 Buick Special Riviera two-door hardtop almost met itself in a crash. Look again—it really is only one car. The Buick was 3 years old with an estimated value of $1,600.00 at the time of the accident. The driver (who was unhurt) fell asleep at the wheel, hit a utility pole directly in the middle, and wrapped the Riviera around the post with the front and back wheels practically meeting. The flipped up hood and the torn back roof added to the two-car illusion.

The damage suffered by this 1956 Nash Rambler Super four-door sedan when it left the road and skidded along the shoulder included having its undercarriage ripped apart and the taillight knocked off.

This 1956 Chevrolet Two-Ten four-door sedan V-8 ran through a stop sign and directly into the path of a truck loaded with topsoil. The impact caused the bed of the truck to lift, spilling dirt onto the Chevy, the road, and the sidewalk.

Awaiting the tow truck is a 1956 Chevrolet Bel Air two-door sedan six-cylinder that crushed a guardrail post after being involved in a head-on collision.

A repairable 1956 Plymouth Savoy two-door hardtop coupe holds the attention of the gentleman long after the other half of this fender bender was towed away. The car sitting in front was struck, which caused it to hurl back into the grille of the Plymouth.

This demolished 1956 Ford Fairlane Victoria two-door hardtop coupe lost its footing. Moving along the highway a bit too quickly, the young driver lost control on a curve and went axle over tin coupe into a cornfield. It took several hours to right the Ford and drag it up the steep bank.

This Chevrolet Two-ten four-door sedan was torn to pieces after side swiping a tree. The rescue crew had to remove the door to free the driver.

A 1957 Chevrolet Two-ten Handyman station wagon with a V-8 engine proved to be less than handy on a foggy, slush-covered road.

A classic 1957 Chevrolet Bel Air two-door hardtop with optional fender skirts, wheel spinner hubcaps, sun visor and dual side mirrors had its face rearranged.

A rough ride through a field took its toll on this 1957 Ford Country Sedan station wagon.

This 1957 Chevrolet Bel Air seems to have a tree growing through it. According to the "V" on both hood and trunk, a 283-cid V-8 engine replaced the standard six-cylinder.

An upended 1957 Nash Ambassador Custom four-door sedan forgot that the rubber is supposed to meet the road. This Ambassador was equipped with a 327-cid V-8 engine and quad headlamps. 1957 was the last year for the big Ambassador.

Photo courtesy of Jack Frey

A 1957 Dodge Coronet (on the left) and a 1958 Dodge Coronet (on the right) decided to tango on a mountain road. 1957 was the first year for the torsion bar front suspension. The new system so impressed *Motor Trend* magazine that they awarded the entire Chrysler Fleet the coveted Car of the Year Award.

A 1957 Pontiac Chieftain two-door sedan. The young driver claimed to have lost control of his car trying to reach home before curfew. The Chieftain engine was stroked to 347 cid at 252 hp with a hydramatic transmission. Note the quintessential 1950s chenille balls hanging from the inside windshield.

The remains of a 1957 Ford Fairlane 500 two-door hardtop. The driver was killed instantly after traveling at a speed estimated at well over 100 mph, losing control of the vehicle, and slamming it into an unyielding tree. Only minutes before the accident, the resident of the home in the background had been mowing the lawn where this twisted mass lies.

This 1957 Chevrolet Two-Ten Townsman station wagon with a 283-cid V-8 (as designated by the "V" on the hood) is the last of a four-car chain reaction. The accident occurred when the driver of the first car stopped on the highway to avoid collision with an illegally passing car. The children seen in the station wagon escaped injury.

Photo courtesy of Jack Frey

This 1957 Oldsmobile Super 88 four-door hardtop snapped two utility poles in a 350-foot skid, which draped live wires across the highway (lower insert). The Oldsmobile left the highway at the start of a curve and crashed into the first pole (number 1), spun around and traveled 200 feet, crashing backwards into the second pole (number 2), traveled an additional 150 feet, and came to rest at the "X" spot. An oncoming 1950 Buick Special Sedanet coupe struck one of the broken poles lying across the road. There were no injuries. Note the 1955 Pontiac Star Chief convertible in the background.

Photo courtesy of *The Williamsport Sun-Gazette*

This 1957 Chevrolet Bel Air four-door sedan was the victim of a slippery, snow-covered road. When the truck crashed broadside into the Chevy, 8-foot oak beams were scattered about the highway like toothpicks.

A 1957 Pontiac Chieftain four-door sedan with a 287-cid V-8 was surprised by a Dodge truck that failed to obey a stop sign. The '57 Chieftain was also offered with a 347-cid V-8 with Tri-power.

This 1957 Ford Fairlane 500 two-door hardtop hit the concrete block garage hard enough to damage the car and crack the walls of the garage. The young boys seem more interested in the optional 312-cid 245-hp V-8 engine than in the condition of the car.

Some days you just can't win. This 1957 Rambler Custom Cross-Country station wagon had insult added to injury. A passing vehicle hit and pushed the Rambler into a utility pole causing moderate damage. Then the Rambler sustained further mutilation when a traffic light fell onto the hood.

A 1957 DeSoto Firedome four-door sedan straddles the sidewalk after being involved in a three-car accident. The second car was towed from the scene after the fire company extinguished a smoldering fire under its dash. The 1955 Pontiac seen in the background was struck as the DeSoto traveled onto the sidewalk.

A 1957 Buick Century two-door hardtop, a brand new car, only a few hours old, is silhouetted by the garage wall hole from whence it came. The Buick crashed through the garage door, crossed inside, skidded atop several beer barrels, then pierced out the other side. The car continued rolling more than 25 feet on the barrels before it came to rest with the front grille imbedded in a second garage wall.

A Ford Fairlane 500 convertible is inspected by the railroad police on the left and insurance investigators on the right. The '57 Ford crashed into a mountain side, swerved across the road, crashed through guardrails, and spun onto the railroad track.

A 1957 Chevrolet Bel Air four-door sedan equipped with a 283-cid V-8 engine, designated by the "V" on the hood, tried to enter the house through the front door.

A 1957 Buick Century two-door hardtop awaits the tow truck after being badly marred. The driver fell asleep, allowing the car to drift off the highway. The driver awoke and swerved back just as he approached a telephone pole, crossed the road and struck an oncoming vehicle.

A 1957 Ford Skyliner retractable hardtop took a hard whack from a 1959 Chevrolet Biscayne. The report stated that fog and rain contributed to poor visibility and slick roads, with "no party at fault." That may very well be a fact, but it is little compensation for the ravaged vehicles.

A 1957 DeSoto Firedome four-door sedan snake danced across a wide shoulder before it came to an abrupt stop against a boulder. Grappling with a slight curve on a wet highway, shown by the oncoming headlights, was beyond this driver's capability. Note the battery jarred from its housing.

This 1958 Edsel Citation hardtop coupe forgot to stop. The Edsel came equipped with a 410-cid V-8 with 345 hp and TeleTouch automatic transmission smack-dab in the middle of the steering wheel.

This 1958 Oldsmobile 88 four-door sedan, the top-selling car for Oldsmobile that year, was totally destroyed. It is interesting to note that a perfect, undamaged 1958 Oldsmobile 88 four-door sedan is parked directly behind the towed wreck.

This 1958 Mercury Monterey Phaeton coupe was unable to stop for the sign due to slick, snow-covered roads. The light pole provided an abrupt alternative. After connecting with the left front fender, the car ricocheted and tapped the right. The '58 was the first Mercury offered with multi-drive transmission.

A 1958 Buick Special four-door sedan snapped two poles that were more than 100 feet apart before veering off the highway in the opposite direction. Riding alone, the driver did not survive the crash.

This 1958 Cadillac Coupe de Ville suffered a hard hit to the rear, but maintains her dignity as she's towed from the scene. Cadillac made the 1958 models available with an air suspension ride, for the added cost of $215, but the system had a tendency to leak!

A 1958 Buick Special Riviera hardtop sedan plunged off a fog-shrouded mountain road after the driver was thrown onto the highway. State police, seen in the background, reported the college student escaped more serious injury by being thrown from the vehicle before it plunged toward a creek.

Photo courtesy of Jack Frey

Fast reaction from local citizens prevented a potential disaster by using a hand-held extinguisher to put out the fire in the carburetor of this 1958 Chevrolet Bel Air four-door sedan.

Neither the cool temperature or the late hour seemed to interfere with the gathering crowd curious to inspect the damage from a nighttime collision involving a 1958 Chevrolet Bel Air straight-six sedan.

A 1958 Chevrolet Bel Air four-door sedan and a 1954 Plymouth Belvedere two-door hardtop collide less than three hours after a new traffic signal went into operation. The Chevy was unable to avoid broadsiding the Plymouth, causing it to slam into a corner meat market.

This 1958 Ford Custom 300 driver explains that a fire just started within the dashboard with no apparent reason. Ice-covered roads delayed the arrival of fire fighters, which was bad news for the car.

A young couple on their honeymoon left a restaurant, seen in the background, and hit a pole in their 1958 Chevrolet Bel Air. The red-faced groom told police that he only intended to give his new wife a little peck on the cheek but, unfortunately, his gesture of affection lasted longer than he anticipated. The next thing he knew they were jolted to a stop by a pole. Luckily, both escaped injury.

A 1958 Ford Ranch station wagon was no match for a tractor. The tractor, being used by the highway department to mow weeds along the road, was struck from behind. There was little or no damage done to the tractor.

Photo courtesy of *The Williamsport Sun-Gazette*

A 1958 Chevrolet Bel Air four-door sedan, a 1958 Ford Fairlane two-door and a 1959 Chevrolet Bel Air four-door sedan crippled traffic on a busy highway when they decided to rumble. Note the Cadillac ambulance in the background.

A 1958 Plymouth Plaza two-door Club sedan was found crashed and abandoned near a municipal airport. Tire marks indicate the car failed to negotiate a curve in the road and struck the tree before it stopped.

This 1958 Buick Riviera hardtop sedan took a nose dive as the driver exited his car and shut the door. The floor of the garage collapsed, dropping the car into the basement. Surprisingly, when the vehicle was pulled from the abyss it had suffered only minor damage.

A 1958 Chevrolet Del Ray sedan left a trail of zigzag tire marks as it sashayed across the highway and onto the shoulder of the road before flipping onto its roof. The driver looks back in apparent disbelief. Undoubtedly, the wet weather had something to do with the road conditions and the spongy shoulder.

A 1958 Ford Custom 300 sedan hit a bridge in the early morning hours while the driver was attempting to miss a deer that ran in front of the car.

Photo courtesy of Jack Frey

Photo courtesy of Jack Frey

A 1958 Edsel Citation four-door hardtop was unoccupied with its 410-cid V-8 motor running when it backed itself down a driveway, banged into the small tree on the left, and eventually slid into its tightly parked position.

This 1958 Cadillac Series 62 hardtop coupe was towed to the yard after a collision that sent four people to the hospital. The Caddie had passed a truck on wet pavement when it went into a skid, swerved into the path of an oncoming vehicle with which it collided and proceeded over an embankment and into a field. Note the Ford tow truck to the right.

A 1958 Ford Custom 300 coupe sustained heavy passenger-side damage and nearly took out a mailbox before coming to a halt.

This 1958 Edsel Citation four-door hardtop had a hard time making it up a grade, so the driver abandoned it overnight. He was going to have a bigger problem when he returned.

A 1959 Chevrolet Bel Air four-door sports sedan proves the vulnerability of a car when confronting a 26-ton locomotive. There were more than 447,000 Bel Airs sold in '59. Many, like this model, with the "flying wing"

This is no way to start a vacation! The driver of this 1959 Chevy Brookwood station wagon was en route to a fishing trip. He blamed a bee flying up his shirtsleeve as being responsible for this mishap. The sudden lurching and braking obviously caused the travel trailer to flip onto its side, lifting the wagon off the road.

A 1959 Chevrolet Impala collided head-on with a 1959 Chevrolet Brookwood station wagon. Both cars were badly damaged, as witnessed by the crowd that quickly gathered.

The inside of this 1959 Buick LeSabre four-door hardtop sedan was not a good place to be after this accident.

A 1959 Ford Custom 300 four-door sedan has a chance meeting with a 1958 Plymouth Belvedere four-door sedan at an otherwise quiet corner. A bright day, dry roads, no leaves on the trees to obstruct the view — one wonders what excuse there could possibly be for wrecking two beautiful cars.

This 1959 Ford Country Fordor station wagon took a sudden ride over an embankment. A 3-year-old child climbed into the family car, tampered with the gearshift. The wagon drifted forward and plunged over the bank and into the stream. The startled child was not injured.

A 1959 Plymouth Sport Fury two-door hardtop unfortunately was at the receiving end of revenge. A group of "angry young men" did not like out-of-towners driving new cars and dating local girls. During a late-night brawl, several prowling hoods forced this car off the street and smashed the windows with ball bats. The visiting young man with his hometown girlfriend sat in a shower of glass particles, but luckily received only slight cuts. The gang members were arrested and served sentences in the county jail.

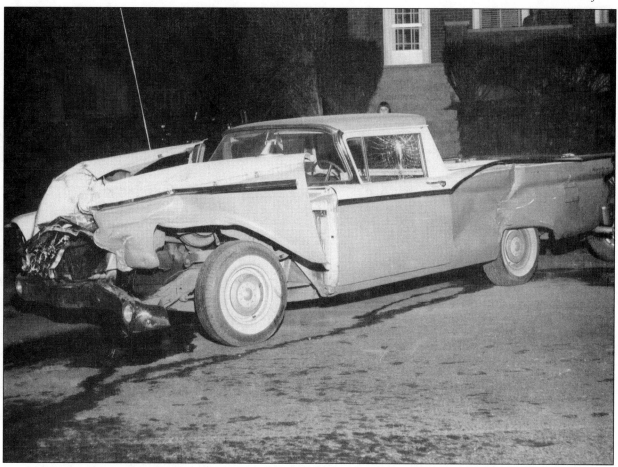

A 1959 Ford Ranchero pickup was badly damaged after a head-on collision. The impact caused the Ranchero to skid backwards some 40 feet before it was stopped by a parked car.

A 1959 Pontiac Catalina tried to make a dramatic entrance. The mishap did not damage the distinctive fender skirts. However, the porch was another story.

This 1959 Ford Custom 300 sedan went airborne after it left the road and smashed into a culvert and hit a tree some 200 feet below.

This 1959 Chevrolet Bel Air confirmed the reality of how treacherous snow-covered roads can be. It's ironic that the Chevy slid head-on into a dump truck full of salt on its way to the highway department to be used to clear the roads.

A 1959 Pontiac Star chief two-door sedan took a hard hit when it was involved in a head on collision. 1959 was the first year for the wide-track.

A 1959 Plymouth Savoy was following too closely to the 1951 Ford. Note the '51 Ford has 1955 chrome added with special fender skirts, full-moon hubcaps, side vent windows, two-tone paint, mud flaps and a sun visor!

A 1959 Ford Fairlane two-door was involved in a horrendous accident with a 1953 Mercury Monterey sedan. Three people lost their lives at a congested junction in north-central Pennsylvania where Rt. 54 crossed Rt. 15, a main artery at the time of the accident, between New York and the south.

Photo courtesy of Jack Frey

A 1959 DeSoto Firesweep four-door sedan driver jammed on the brakes and swerved in an effort to miss a young boy chasing after his dog. The child fared only slightly better than the car — his mother whacked him as she hurried to apologize to the driver. The child is rubbing his backside as his astonished friend watches. All witnessed by the neighborhood watch group.

A 1959 Ford Fairlane 500 Skyliner retractable hardtop is only a distorted shell of the dazzling beauty it once was.

A 1955 Chevrolet Bel Air two-door sedan and 1959 Oldsmobile Super 88 Holiday four-door hardtop had a bad mix-up on a busy highway.

A 1948 Chevrolet Fleetline two-door stopped for the stop sign then entered the intersection, forming an unpleasant union with a 1960 Pontiac Bonneville convertible.

A 1950 Dodge Meadowbrook four-door sedan comes together with a 1960 Ford Galaxie Sunliner convertible. How many men does it take to examine a crumpled fender? At least eight!

A 1954 Plymouth Savoy sedan tapped a 1966 Pontiac GTO convertible. Both then posed perfectly to have their picture taken.

Photo courtesy of The Williamsport Sun-Gazette

A 1955 Mercury was rear-ended by a 1961 Rambler Cross Country station wagon. With not another car or person in sight, you would think that an accident could have been avoided.

A 1955 Ford Fairlane 500 with a 292 V-8 has taken, and delivered, a solid blow during a run-in with a 1961 Chevrolet Brookwood station wagon.

Photo courtesy of *The Lock Haven Express*

A 1955 Chevrolet Two-Ten four-door sedan was t-boned by a 1964 Ford Galaxie 500 Sunliner convertible coupe.

Photo courtesy of *The Lock Haven Express*

A 1957 Studebaker Silver Hawk, offered in '57 with either a six-cylinder or a V-8, neglected to stop at a red light and was pushed into a utility pole subsequent to being hit by a 1965 Oldsmobile 88 sedan.

A 1957 Ford Custom 300 four-door sedan flips its lid when smacked by a 1960 Chevrolet Impala.

Photo courtesy of *The Williamsport Sun-Gazette*

A 1957 Buick Super driver sideswiped his neighbor driving a 1961 Oldsmobile Dynamic 88 convertible. The Olds pulled out of his driveway when he caught his next-door neighbor's fender as he returned home from work.

A 1958 Pontiac Chieftain and 1961 Mercury Comet station wagon flipped for each other.

A 1959 Chevrolet Impala was destroyed during a head-on collision with a 1962 Ford Sunliner convertible.

A 1959 Ford Fairlane 500 four-door sedan lost its integrity in a head-on collision, then went on to slide its rear into a 1960 Ford Fairlane 500 Town sedan. Note the gas station in the background — gas was 29 cents a gallon.

A 1959 Chevrolet Bel Air four-door sedan was jammed by a 1962 Mercury Colony Park station wagon. A local police officer seems to have everything under control.

1960s

The social, cultural and political climate changed in ways that even today leave us bewildered, but the vehicles of the 1960s will forever be the machines of boastful charisma and hopeful optimism. Moscow released a directive stating, "The capitalist, free market response to the automobile has been unscientific, even irrational." The U.S. car buyer's response was "Yeah Baby."

The unscientific Barracuda and the irrational Corvette put the country's youth first. We cheerfully sacrificed the chrome and fins of the '50s to embrace the exciting technology that tested the boundaries of convention. Detroit was at its most imaginative and receptive, providing vehicles of pleasure with personality and distinction that were a kick to drive and a joy to look at and listen to. The rear-engine Corvair, the front-wheel-drive Tor-

onado, and Pontiac LeMans with rear trans-axle and overhead-cam six were definitely not our mothers' cars.

The decade started out uncomplicated with more disposable income and an Easy Street that stretched from Boston to L.A. But as women's skirts got shorter and men's hair grew longer, the times they were a changin'. Richard Petty and his Hemi-powered Belvedere racked up one of the greatest one-year performances in motor sports history, winning 27 NASCAR races, including 10 in a row. Beatlemania hit a fevered pitch when the British foursome made its first appearance on "The Ed Sullivan Show." The British invasion continued with the Rolling Stones, The Who, The Animals, and the Dave Clark Five. Detroit also contributed to the swing with the Shangri-Las' "Leader of the

A tattered Checker taxicab failed to stop when everyone else did. It's doubtful the cabbie collected a tip after this incident.

Pack," Jan & Dean's "Dead Man's Curve" and "The Little Old Lady from Pasadena." F.D.A. approved the birth control pill, the U.S. Circuit Court of Appeals ruled that D. H. Lawrence's *Lady Chatterley's Lover* was not obscene but in fact literary art. The Berlin Wall was built. President Kennedy ordered Russian ballistic missiles out of Cuba, Nikita Khrushchev blinked and we all sighed with the peaceful end of the Cuban Missile Crisis. The United States sent economic, social and military aid to a small Southeast Asian country that few had heard of called Vietnam.

Many believe "the end of innocence" came suddenly shortly after noon in Dallas on November 22, 1963, when President Kennedy was assassinated. The fabric of America took another hit when The Rev. Martin Luther King was shot in Memphis and Sen. Robert F. Kennedy was mortally wounded in Los Angeles.

Pop culture reflected the restless turbulence of the country as movie watchers beat a path to the theaters to watch *Rosemary's Baby, Planet of the Apes,* and *In Cold Blood*. And in *Bullitt*, Steve McQueen put his '68 Ford Mustang GT 390 to the test on the streets of San Francisco.

GM chairman Donner and president Roche embarrassed themselves and the industry as a whole, appearing evasive or uninformed when grilled by a Congressional committee on auto safety. Their pitiful performance contributed to the government's intensified efforts to mandate safety requirements. National Highway Safety Bureau, a thorn in the side of Detroit, was initiated and headed by Dr. William Haddan Jr., author of the Federal Motor Vehicle Safety Standards. These standards established a minimum safety code that all vehicles were required to meet; such as energy-absorbing frames, front head rests and side impact door beams. Ford endured a crippling 61-day strike. *Highway Research Record* published an article describing "balloon-like air bags in passenger cars that would inflate automatically upon impact."

The GM research lab received a $493,000 grant to evaluate and develop a "highway route-guidance system" that would direct motorists to their destination. Inventor Don Dean devised a steering wheel that gave a sleepy driver intermittent electrical shocks. Jody Carr, a Chicago auto columnist, advised women to learn more about cars, but added, "I don't propose that we discard our aprons for overalls."

In 1969 Neil Armstrong became the first human to walk on the moon. Here on Earth, 400,000 walked through the mud on a farm in Woodstock, New York, and Sen. Ted Kennedy plunged his car from a bridge at Chappaquiddick Island. It was a sign of the times when Ralph Nader's book *Unsafe At Any Speed* was more chic than *Car and Driver*.

A 1960 Oldsmobile 88 Celebrity four-door sedan tried to take a shortcut through a neighbor's yard. The 88 Celebrity was Oldsmobile's most popular model in 1960 with 76,377 units built.

A 1960 Ford Country station wagon glided into and along the side of a bridge when the motorist fell asleep. This was Ford's most popular wagon with over 78,000 built in 1960.

A 1960 Ford Starliner two-door hardtop left the road and shattered several makeshift guard posts before tumbling onto its roof. Note the International delivery truck in the background filled with milk cans.

A 1960 Chevrolet four-door Impala sedan with a 283-cid V-8 sits subdued and broken among other abused and discarded vehicles. This once-beautiful Chevy was pushed to speeds of over 90 mph along the highway before a devastating confrontation with a telephone pole.

This 1960 Ford Galaxie Starliner hardtop coupe was used as a ramp by the truck in the background to clear the guardrails and lunge over the riverbank.

A 1960 Chevrolet Impala kissed the end of a bridge. Judging by the reaction of the onlookers, the damage to car and driver was not tragic.

This 1960 Oldsmobile Super 88 Holiday Sport sedan was the subject of great discussion. The reporting officer looks as though he would rather be about anywhere except standing beside a wrecked Olds listening to not only the driver explaining what happened, but about a dozen kids all with their own opinion.

This 1960 Mercury Montclair four-door sedan took a tumble. The woman, unhurt but badly shaken, told police that she was blinded by the sun as it reflected off the windshield of a passing car. She jerked the wheel and slammed on the brakes, which caused the car to go into a ditch and overturn.

A 1960 Buick Electra 225 took a young couple first to church and then to tragedy. The car was struck by a train, spun around 22 feet and came to rest as shown near a utility pole. Since the time of this catastrophe, the railroads have adopted a policy for several whistle warnings and a much slower speed — not to exceed 30 mph — while going through populated areas.

A 1960 Ford Galaxie Town sedan four-door proved once again that "rubber-necking" is a sport enjoyed by the young and old alike.

The driver of this 1960 Oldsmobile Dynamic 88 Celebrity was surprised by a truck on its way to deliver powdered fertilizer. The bending of metal was only the beginning of the Olds's problems. The truck dropped several bags of its dubious cargo, dusting the car, the driver and entire area with the noxious powder.

A 1960 Chevrolet Brookwood four-door station wagon demonstrates that it is far more appropriate to go over a bridge than under one. It's hard to figure how the car got in this position.

A 1960 Pontiac Star Chief four-door sedan was another victim of the battered and scared tree silhouetted on the right. The tree, located on a sharp curve along a rural New York road, had been responsible for numerous deaths. The curse began in 1929 when four young men were killed when their car hit the tree, a month later another lost his life, and the carnage continued with many other single fatalities throughout the years until the May evening in 1961 when this accident occurred.

A 1960 Oldsmobile Dynamic 88 Holiday hardtop four-door sedan paid the consequence for sibling rivalry. According to the report, the mother explained that her sons were quibbling over a toy. She turned around for a second to settle the disagreement and the next thing she knew the car was being stopped by a tree.

A 1960 Plymouth Fury convertible and a 1969 Pontiac LeMans were both totaled in a head-on collision. The Plymouth rounded a curve and drifted over the middle of the road. The tight squeeze from a mountain to the right and a steep cliff to the left allowed for very little maneuverability.

A 1960 Chevrolet Corvair Club coupe takes a hit. Note this was the first year for Chevrolet's Corvair.

A 1960 Oldsmobile 88 four-door sedan mowed down a fence row, but seems not to have suffered much for its driver's blunder.

A 1960 Pontiac Catalina convertible coupe is scarred from the force of a blow that destroyed the left rear quarter panel and shoved the front into the guardrail post.

This 1960 Ford Falcon has been paralyzed by the sacrifice of a left front wheel. Note: Falcon scored big in 1960 with 435,671 built in its first year.

A 1960 Dodge Matador sedan was hit and injured by a 1947 souped-up Studebaker pickup. You can almost feel the pain of the sorrowful Studebaker with its walloped eye, sagging mouth, and ripped, crumpled face.

A 1960 Pontiac Catalina Safari station wagon is inspected by the sharply attired police officer that arrived on his tri-wheel cycle. The skid marks track the path taken by the Pontiac as it rolled along and cut across the street before being hung-up on the thigh-high stump of a utility pole it had sheared.

Photos courtesy of *The Williamsport Sun-Gazette*

A 1960 Cadillac two-door hardtop, the big, proud heavyweight highway baron, has suffered the indignity of a crinkled rear quarter panel. I took a hit hard enough to knock off its hubcaps.

This 1961 Ford Thunderbird convertible had its wings clipped as it tried to fly through a busy intersection.

A 1961 Oldsmobile 88 two-door hardtop became a one-car hardtop after this highway mishap. The highway patrolman seems to be taking inventory of missing parts.

A 1961 Chevrolet four-door Bel Air has been towed to the back of the garage with the rest of the junk —a sad ending to for such a fine automobile.

A 1960 Ford Fairlane Town sedan exhibits a classic endorsement for "no-fault insurance." The narrow makeshift bridge across this gully would have been treacherous under ideal conditions. When snow-covered, it was an accident waiting to happen.

The three occupants miraculously suffered only minor injuries when thrown from this 1961 Dodge Lancer station wagon as it tumbled down a mountainside before coming to rest against a tree.

A 1961 Plymouth Savoy sedan found a final resting place within the walls of a garage. Note the "Safety Award" hanging behind the car.

The 1961 Chevrolet Impala was being driven by a young girl with a brand new driver's learner permit. She explained to the police officer that she became excited when she saw oncoming traffic and stepped on the gas by mistake, bumping a 1963 Cadillac. Note the police motorcycle on the right and the Ford Econoline emergency van.

Photo courtesy of *The Williamsport Sun-Gazette*

This 1961 Dodge Lancer 770 station wagon evoked such cavalier responses from the bystanders because in this case the damages far exceeded the injuries. The wagon was struck by a train and thrown 30 feet, with the very lucky driver escaping with only a minor injury.

A 1961 Chevrolet Corvair Club coupe forgot to keep its feet firmly on the ground. The spectators to this late-night entertainment enjoyed having their picture taken almost as much as witnessing the Corvair's dilemma.

Photo courtesy of *The Lock Haven Express*

A 1961 Ford Galaxie Sunliner convertible chose an unconventional method of getting attention. The young men in the photo at least managed to keep a sense of humor.

A 1961 Chrysler New Yorker two-door hardtop was no match for even a small tree.

This 1961 Dodge Phoenix two-door hardtop whacked a utility pole with such force that pieces of wood were scattered over the street and nearby field.

A 1962 Oldsmobile Super 88 sports sedan jumped the curb and crashed into a storefront. When my 8-year-old nephew, Jordan, saw this photo, he said, "Look Uncle Bud, the original drive-thru store!"

This 1962 Ford Galaxie 500 four-door sedan looks to be emerging from the house. Actually, after running a stop sign and colliding with another vehicle, the car traveled 30 feet across the lawn, spun around and came to rest against the hedges. The surprised homeowners were just inside the bay window reading the paper at the time of the accident.

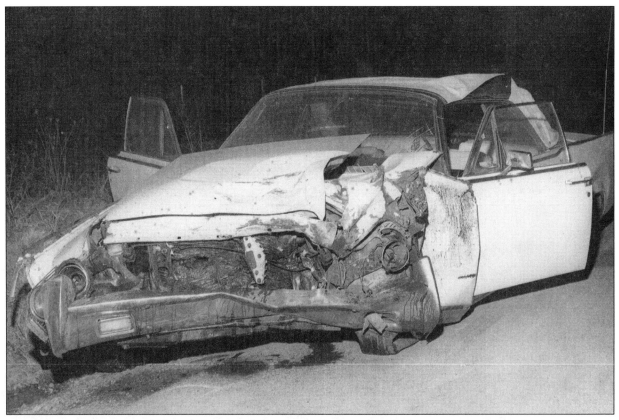

A 1962 Lincoln Continental four-door convertible with suicide doors shows what can happen when the driver is concentrating more on eating a hamburger than driving. The driver of this big, beautiful boat reported that his greasy hand slipped off the steering wheel as he entered the curve leading to a bridge, causing the "ship to hit the span."

This 1962 Chevrolet Impala four-door sedan was involved in a two-car collision. After colliding with the other vehicle and crumpling the front, the Chevy swung around and damaged its rear.

A 1962 Chevrolet Impala Super Sport may not appear to be badly damaged, but it was the final ride for one woman. At a double crossing, a patient woman waited as one train headed. After it passed, she proceeded through the gate at the same time a west-bound train approached from the opposite direction.

Photo courtesy of Jack Frey

This 1962 Chevrolet Corvair 900 Monza convertible looks to have backed up to the window for an oil change. Remember, with the engine in the back, the trunk that is open is actually the hood.

A f1962 Chevrolet Bel Air station wagon and a 1962 Oldsmobile Dynamic 88 Holiday hardtop coupe battled for the same piece of asphalt. This battle had no winners.

This 1962 AMC Rambler Rebel Custom four-door sedan was well protected with the U.S. Army swarming in to investigate.

A driver in a 1962 Chevrolet Biscayne two-door sedan with a 327 engine was traveling home from work when a car sped out of a side street and clobbered him with such force that the driver's door was completely knocked off and thrown some 150 feet. The Chevy continued on and leaped the curb before coming to a stop. Somehow, the 1967 Chevrolet Impala parked at the curb remained untouched.

A 1962 Chevrolet Corvair 900 Monza convertible coupe pulls back its upper lip and snarls after ramming into the side of the mountain.

This 1962 Mercury Meteor coupe was sitting in the parking lot of an adult bookstore when it was struck by a runaway truck.

A 1962 Pontiac Catalina Safari station wagon could not avoid sliding into a 1962 Ford Falcon four-door sedan at an intersection covered with an icy slush. The driver of the 1963 Ford Thunderbird in the background approaches slowly while trying to miss this little gathering.

A 1962 AMC Classic sedan sucker punched a 1965 Chevrolet Bel Air station wagon (background) as it moved along the highway.

This 1962 Ford Falcon has tires worn as bare as a baby's butt. Evidently, the rubber just could not hold the Ford to the ground.

A 1962 Chevrolet Bel Air two-door sedan looks like its driver apparently didn't read the "Bridge Is Out" sign. Actually, the driver drove down the bank on the work road and into the river until running out of luck at the middle pier.

A 1963 Ford Galaxie ends up in the weeds as a bystander surveys the scene.

A 1963 Ford Falcon Deluxe four-door sedan jumped the curb, crossed the lawn, tackled a pine tree and knocked down the end of the porch.

Photo courtesy of *The Lock Haven Express*

This 1963 Pontiac Bonneville Vista four-door hardtop equipped with a 389-cid V-8 engine was traveling at a high rate of speed when the driver lost control, left the highway, and slammed into a tree, causing the door to fly off. Note that the stacked headlights, which were new in '63, were untouched on the driver's side.

This 1963 Plymouth Belvedere four-door sedan was pushed 300 feet by a train that was backing up. The driver admitted to seeing and hearing the signal that alerted drivers and pedestrians to a train in the process of "coupling." The driver, having lived his entire life in the small railroading town, was familiar with switches and couplings, but decided to take his chances by ignoring the dangers. Although no people were injured, the Plymouth certainly paid the price for his poor judgment.

A 1963 Chevrolet Biscayne took a hard hit before traveling through a field. The fin peeking from behind the Chevy revealed that a '58 Cadillac was no doubt the dancing partner in this collision.

A 1963 Chevrolet II Nova 400 four-door sedan was the source of amusement for several young men. Luckily, no one was injured when the math teacher jumped the curb and bolted into the school. The teacher was not available for comment.

A 1963 Chrysler Newport sedan was backed into while sitting in an employee parking lot. It is assumed that a delivery truck was responsible for this amount of damage, but no note was left and at the time of the report no one had witnessed the accident, which was officially listed as a hit and run.

Photo courtesy of Jack Frey

A 1963 Ford Fairlane 500 two-door sedan with a 289 V-8, (previous page), literally exploded upon impact. What must have been going through this person head as he accelerated, lost control and slammed into a tree in front of a college dormitory this night? One witness told of a thundering rumble shaking the ground as the car first slammed against the tree and great sparks shot as the fractured front end whirled toward the building over 200 feet up the hill. Note the can of Colt 45 beer in the grass in the third photograph — possibly a clue to the cause of the horrifying accident.

Photo courtesy of Jack Frey

A 1963 Chevrolet II Nova 300 Series sedan knocked over a gasoline pump, shattered the storefront glass, and damaged merchandise. The calamity started in the street in front of the Firestone store when the Nova collided with a truck, jumped the curb and proceeded into the station. The fire department covered the area with foam as a precautionary measure.

A 1963 Chevrolet Bel Air station wagon scored a bull's-eye hit on the side of this house. No one was seriously injured, but the woman of the house, working in the kitchen, was shocked when one more dropped in for dinner.

The driver of a 1963 Chevrolet Impala Super Sport two-door hardtop with a 327-cid V-8 somehow missed seeing a tractor-trailer truck that was directly in front of them. Note the spinner hubcaps and chenille balls hanging inside the windshield.

A 1963 Ford Galaxie four-door sedan hammered through the side of wooden house. Judging from the appearance of the Ford, the driver may have been searching for an all-night car wash.

A 1963 Ford Falcon Deluxe station wagon was sporting a nice scar after a fender bender.

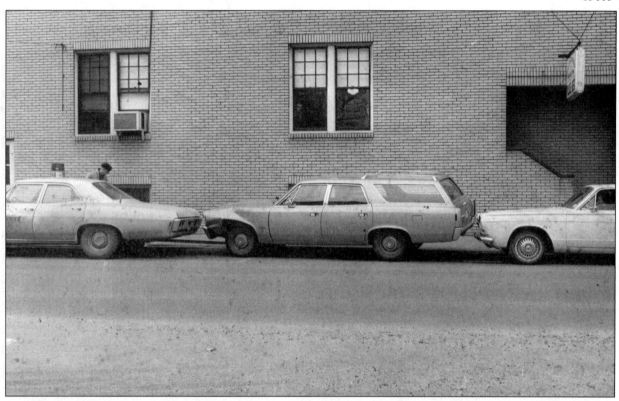

This 1963 Dodge Dart 270 Series sedan's driver was really having a bad day. Not only did it run into a 1967 AMC Rambler Rebel 550 station wagon, pushing it into a 1968 Chevrolet Biscayne four-door Police cruiser, it all happened right in front of the police station. That is not the end of the story. The driver had stopped at the station to pay a parking fine they received the previous day.

A 1963 Oldsmobile Dynamic 88 made the sparks fly from the power company pole. A car full of excited high school fans were leaving the football field after a spectacular win when, for some reason that nobody could explain, the car suddenly went off the road and struck the pole. It appears as if the entire fan club moved from the bleachers to the accident.

A 1963 Mercury Monterey Breezeway sedan left a twisty mountain road, flew through the air and plunged head first into the turbulent stream, stubbing its nose and discarding its dumbfounded occupants into the frigid waters.

This 1963 Chevrolet Nova 300 station wagon was an unwelcome visitor. The car burst through the end of a mobile home, shattered the wall, fixtures and furniture, including a bed in which the resident was sleeping, and pinned her beneath the car. The sleeping victim, although badly shaken, was not seriously injured.

A 1963 Ford Galaxie 500 sedan sports a bruise after being blind-sided.

The driver of a 1963 Mercury Meteor Custom coupe jumped the low-profile curb to knock at the door of this bungalow. Note the 1963 Chevrolet police car that came to take the new mother and baby home.

This 1963 Chevrolet Biscayne sedan left the road, hit a post, then coasted to a stop in a cornfield.

A 1963 Dodge 440 Series station wagon was struck from the side when the participants had their vision obstructed by a heavy early morning fog.

A 1963 Pontiac Catalina convertible coupe successfully completed a sharp curve, but then hit a patch of ice, broke through a pole, then crashed head-on into this large tree.

A 1963 Chevrolet Impala sport coupe demonstrated just how dangerous tree-lined roads can be. A 19-year-old man was thrown from the car upon impact with the tree and was killed. His bride of two months was seriously hurt, but survived.

A 1963 Chevrolet Impala two-door hardtop was bulldozed by an oncoming truck. A more severe accident was avoided when the driver of the Chevy realized that the truck was obviously heading straight for him and drove onto the shoulder. The truck driver later admitted to falling asleep at the wheel.

A 1963 Dodge 330 two-door coupe was less fortunate off the track than on.

A 1963 Chrysler 300 shows the scars received from a storm of rocks that showered down upon it. The owner holds the rock that flew through the front windshield.

A 1963 Chevrolet 900 Monza two-door coupe tried to put a pole in its trunk. With the air-cooled engine in the rear, the front end provided ample storage space, but not quite enough for a telephone pole.

A 1963 Dodge Polara four-door hardtop was sacrificed on a notoriously dangerous length of highway. The straight, open stretch invites speed and recklessness that often results in this type of catastrophe.

This 1963 Chevrolet II Nova 300 four-door sedan was once a thing of beauty. Polished chrome and waxed hood gleamed under the lights in a Chevy showroom window. The force of this impact shoved the engine off its mounting and onto the floor of the diver's compartment, which suffered as badly as the exterior.

A 1963 Chevrolet Impala two-door hardtop had a brutal showdown with a 1968 Ford Mustang convertible. Both vehicles paid the ultimate price for their drivers' mistakes.

A 1963 Chevrolet II Nova SS convertible with a six-cylinder engine met it match at an intersection.

A 1963 Oldsmobile F-185 two-door coupe tried in vain to forge a road where none existed. The Oldsmobile was struck by a passing freight train, but was only slightly damaged on the right rear quarter panel.

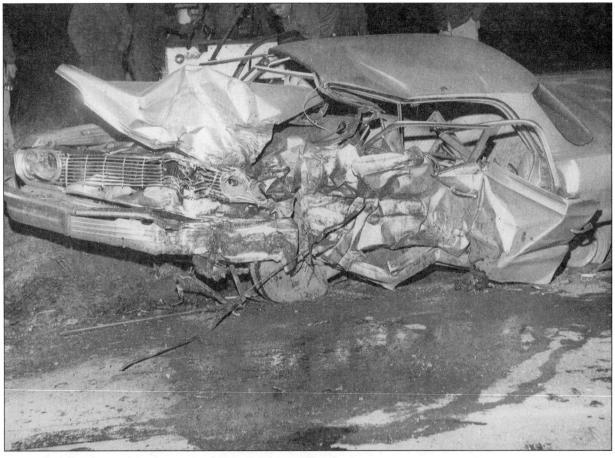

A 1964 Chevrolet Biscayne four-door sedan's shredded remnants rest upon the embankment along a heavily traveled country road. The Chevy was being driven by young girl returning home from late-night babysitting when it collided with a second car. It took rescue workers more than an hour to remove the critically injured girl.

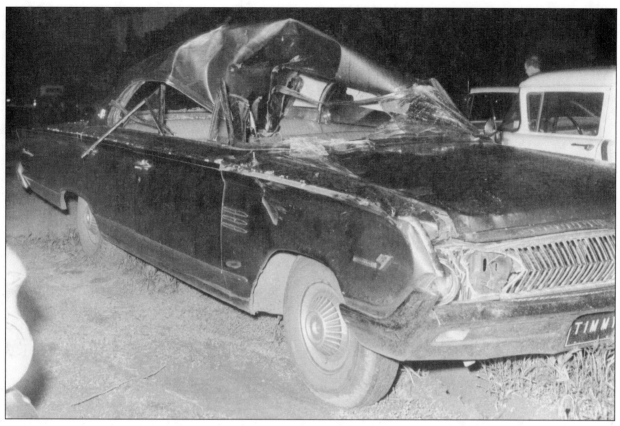

This 1964 Mercury Marauder, designated by the flag emblem on the front fender, nearly became a convertible.

Photo courtesy of *The Lock Haven Express*

A 1964 Chevrolet Impala Sport two-door hardtop coupe, (previous page), ripped apart a Volkswagen. The crumpled mass that was once the VW's front section remained at the point of impact while the rear flew several hundred yards in one direction. The Chevy's dislodged 327 V-8 engine, along with other barely recognizable car parts, was scattered along the highway.

Photo courtesy of *The Lock Haven Express*

A 1964 Ford Thunderbird Landau hardtop coupe is inspected after being towed to the garage. The driver plowed into a truck that had stopped.

A 1964 Ford Country station wagon driver had a bad night after he rear-ended the tail of a slow-moving lowboy truck. Note that there was no damage done to the hood.

A 1964 Plymouth Sport Fury two-door hardtop was in trouble coming and going. A car that failed to stop for a stop sign kissed the left front and rear of the Plymouth.

A 1964 Ford Mustang and a 1966 Ford Mustang engage in some horseplay. Note the optional vinyl roof on the '64.

A 1964 Buick LeSabre sedan was in no position to clear this ditch.

This 1964 Chevrolet Bel Air four-door sedan was destroyed, as was the life of the driver.

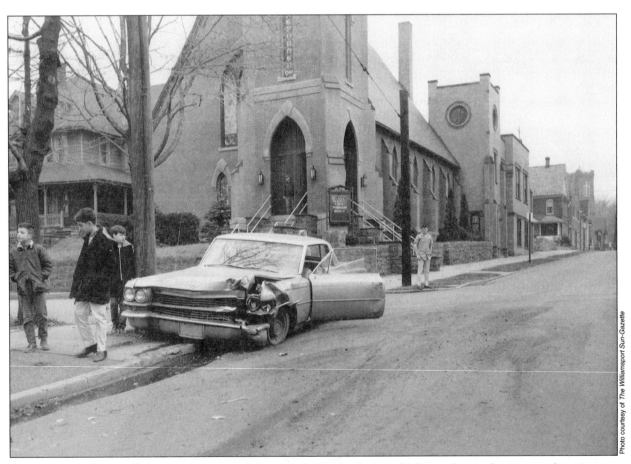

A 1964 Cadillac DeVille hardtop coupe received a crumpled fender from a vehicle traveling in the opposite direction.

A 1964 Chevrolet Bel Air four-door sedan sits beaten and bruised among other relics, including a 1962 Pontiac Tempest station wagon.

This 1964 Ford Custom 500 four-door sedan sat patiently awaiting repairs at a body shop, only to find out it's been totaled from a less-than-cordial reception from a retaining wall.

At first glance, this 1964 Ford Galaxie XL convertible coupe may seem normal, but one look at the rear reveals significant damage.

A 1964 Buick LeSabre four-door sedan's driver seems to be trying to explain to the officer why he rammed the 1964 Dodge 440 sedan, while its driver, hands on hips, clearly disagrees.

A runaway 1964 Chrysler Imperial Crown four-door hardtop caused some uproar in the neighborhood by catapulting into the house and office of the township constable!

A 1964 Plymouth Barracuda fastback coupe was the pride and joy of a young man for a grand total of two days (note the temporary tags) before it became embroiled in a nasty run-in with a 1969 Pontiac LeMans coupe. Note the add-on chrome wheels on the Barracuda.

This 1964 Oldsmobile Starfire convertible coupe experienced a bumpy ride over a pipe down the middle of a bridge.

This unlucky 1964 AMC American sedan traveled down a 7 percent grade when suddenly the brakes locked, causing the AMC to dig into the bank and flip onto its roof.

A 1964 Chevrolet Bel Air four-door sedan had a shocking experience when leaving the road and hitting a pole. A transformer, jarred loose from the impact, fell through the window. The terrified driver sat perfectly still as the car continued across the highway and came to a stop in the brush.

A 1965 Chevrolet Biscayne four-door was one of the members of a two-car collision at a four-way stop sign that two drivers chose to ignore. After coming together with the 1964 Dodge Dart 270 two-door hardtop, seen in the background, the Chevrolet continued on until being stopped by an unforgiving utility pole.

A 1965 Ford Mustang GT convertible is missing its 289 V-8. The young driver was only a half-mile from home when he drove into a utility pole and was killed instantly.

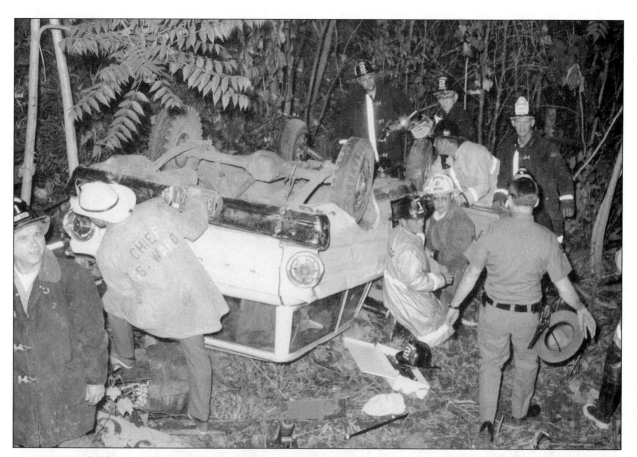

A 1965 Ford Falcon two-door station wagon has ample attention from one of the many brave volunteer emergency crews that respond to duty no matter the hour, location, or conditions. The countless lives they save, as they did in this case, stand as testimony to their dedication.

A 1965 AMC Rambler Rebel 550 sedan was drawn to 1961 Pontiac Tempest sedan, which in return was forced onto the sidewalk and into a tree.

A 1965 Pontiac Tempest Custom convertible coupe cozies up to a 1971 AMC Hornet coupe while a Dodge Challenger is towed away.

A 1965 Chevrolet Impala hardtop has been twisted every which way but straight. This poor, pathetic Chevy has no alternative but the bone yard.

The driver in this 1965 Oldsmobile Dynamic Delta Holiday four-door sedan hit a bridge as he attempted to dodge an out-of-control truck. Alternating altercations between the stone wall and utility pole account for the damages.

A 1965 Ford Mustang convertible hit the guardrail post with such force that the air filter and cover were sent flying.

This 1965 Buick Wildcat convertible coupe could not resist tapping the rear of a 1965 Chevrolet Impala four-door hardtop. Note the Chevrolet Malibu coupe with chrome rear wheels visible behind the Impala.

A 1965 Plymouth Barracuda Fastback coupe received a spanking hard enough to spin it around and knock a parking meter over.

A 1965 Chevrolet Biscayne sedan demonstrates again that a big tree will not give an inch to a car.

A 1965 Chevrolet Chevelle Malibu hardtop coupe chased a school bus off the road. Luckily, no one was injured when the driver of the car suffered a diabetic shock and drove in front of the school bus and continued on into the ditch.

Photo courtesy of Jack Frey

A 1965 Ford Mustang hardtop coupe (background) sent a 1971 AMC whirling over the curb.

A 1965 Dodge Coronet station wagon and a 1970 Chevrolet Monte Carlo two-door hardtop coupe demonstrate that mishaps can and do happen on bright sunny days for no apparent reason, except carelessness.

A 1965 Mercury Monterey four-door sedan had an evening engagement with a tree.

A 1965 Buick LeSabre four-door hardtop branded a pony in the rear hindquarter. The 1966 Ford Mustang hardtop coupe is definitely headed to the body shop.

This 1965 Ford Falcon station wagon succeeded where the hunters had failed. The two young men reportedly had spent the day deer hunting. Their efforts were fruitless and they were returning home. When a deer jumped from a ledge in front of the car, it became entangled between the right front wheel and the frame. The car, which could not be steered, struck a guard post, which prevented a 50-foot drop into the river.

A 1965 Ford Custom four-door sedan was given a final ride by a tow truck. A sudden side impact with a utility pole was enough to dislodge the seat, which rests on the hood.

This 1965 Ford Mustang was a lost cause after bulldozing into the side of a mountain and bursting into flames.

A 1966 Chevrolet Caprice Estate station wagon hit a 1962 Ford Sunliner convertible. The Caprice came with a 283 V-8 as standard, but offered a 427 V-8 as an option. The '62 Ford came with a 292 V-8, but offered a 406 V-8 as an option.

A 1966 Chevrolet Biscayne four-door six cylinder station wagon was slightly t-boned by a VW bug (far left). Note the company name on the door — it didn't seem to be "Protective" this day!

A big 1966 Oldsmobile Starfire two-door hardtop gives new meaning to "stop and smell the flowers." The building seems to have suffered greater indignities than the Olds.

This 1966 Oldsmobile Delta 88 four-door sedan came to a hard stop at the spreading maple tree.

A 1966 Ford Galaxie 500 four-door sedan was sitting in the wrong place when a train dumped its load of coal.

A 1966 Ford Mustang hardtop coupe with a 289-cid V-8 engine received a kick in the front end, but the driver was able to jump in and ride this pony home.

A 1966 Ford Galaxie 500 sedan, by all appearances, had little cooperation from the front disc brakes that were a new added option in '66.

A 1966 Ford Mustang hardtop coupe was left in shambles after a brutal wreck. The young driver passed several cars, traveled along the berm, spun back onto the highway, crossed diagonally and violently wrapped the car around a tree.

This 1966 Ford Mustang hardtop coupe had its face rearranged, but it doesn't appear to be a total loss.

This 1966 Dodge Coronet driver had your classic lazy afternoon wreck. A simple fender-bender with a fence.

A 1966 Plymouth Fury four-door hardtop and 1968 Plymouth Road Runner hardtop coupe bumped noses. The "Runner" came around the corner, surprising the Fury driver at the crest of a hill.

A 1966 Dodge Charger two-door fastback hardtop coupe screamed down the road until coming up short against an opponent that put a quick end to its travels.

This 1966 Mercury Comet 202 two-door coupe sits battered and bruised in the shade of the tree it recently belted. By the appearance of the scarred trunk, this is not the first casualty this tree has seen.

Photo courtesy of Jack Frey

This 1967 Mercury Cougar reached the end of the road on a snowy winter day.

This 1967 Pontiac GTO two-door hard top was driven to the police station after hitting a pole.

A 1967 Pontiac GTO rolled over twice before coming to a halt in a grassy field. It is painful to see this once noble road warrior so badly injured. 1967 marked the end of the first-generation body style for the celebrated GTO.

Little is recognizable on this 1967 Chevrolet Corvette Sting Ray convertible after a high-speed wreck.

Photo courtesy of Jack Frey

Photo courtesy of Jack Frey

A 1967 Pontiac Catalina and a 1971 Ford Maverick skidded into one another on a busy, rain-slick highway.

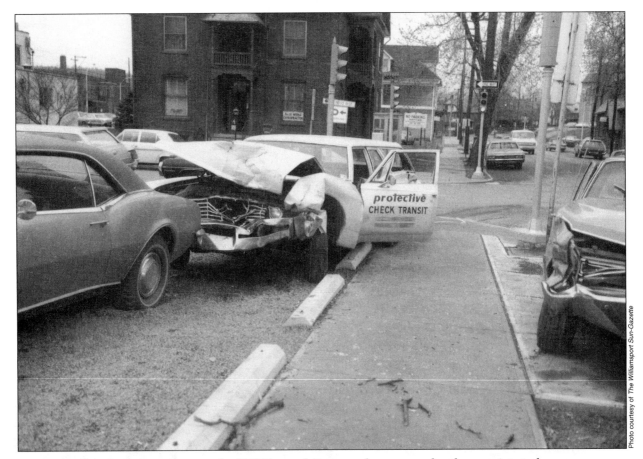

A 1967 Chevrolet Biscayne wagon and a 1968 Plymouth Fury two-door meet and exchange paint at a busy intersection.

A 1967 Chevrolet Impala four-door sedan toppled into a ditch when the driver suffered a heart attack while driving. The gentleman recovered from the misadventure. The car did not.

A 1967 Ford Country sedan station wagon, a 1969 Ford Custom Ranch station wagon, and a 1964 Chevrolet C-10 truck crossed paths at the same time, and none emerged unscathed.

A 1967 Chevrolet Corvette convertible with a 427 engine, a once proud and noble beast, has been reduced to a mangled and mutilated mass of fiberglass. The car would be a valuable collector car today, had it survived.

This 1967 AMC Rambler Rebel 770 coupe experienced a punishing defeat at the trunk of a steadfast tree. A flawed attempt to speed around a menacing curve ended in tragedy.

The owner of this mashed 1967 Ford Falcon Futura coupe was not doing too well this year. The bumper sticker shows they chose to back a losing ticket, while at the same time '67 was also a losing year for Falcon with sales falling to an all-time low of 64,000 units.

A 1968 Plymouth Belvedere sedan was struck by a milk truck that was making a delivery to the elementary school just down the street. The poor young driver now had to go home and explain to his parents the damage done to their car while he was driving his little brother and friends to school.

A 1968 Pontiac Catalina four-door sedan elbowed a 1972 Oldsmobile 98, then went nose first into a maple tree.

A 1967 Chevrolet Impala four-door hardtop crashed with a 1963 Ford Galaxie 500 two-door coupe as it pulled from a parking lot on a cool, bleak fall day.

This 1968 Chevrolet Camaro SS 350 had a serious run-in with a bridge support.

This 1968 Ford Mustang hardtop coupe is going to need some new rubber, glass, and sheet metal after whacking a stoplight post.

A 1968 Dodge Charger R/T coupe received a cold reception from a river swollen from a spring thaw. Racing down a mountain road, the young driver was unable to correct a sudden spin that resulted in a nasty run-in with a tree. The car bounced down a steep embankment and into the icy waters.

A 1968 Plymouth Road Runner two-door hardtop with a 383 V-8 has been ripped to pieces. Although the particulars of this accident have been lost, there are several hints to this woeful outcome. Speed is an obvious culprit, evident from the amount of damage sustained. The Hooker header exhaust system and the Detroit connection stickers still readable implies a desire for a "souped-up" car. Along with the catastrophic collision, a scorched hood reveals a carburetor fire.

A 1968 Buick Skylark four-door sedan with an optional vinyl roof was stopped by a Chevrolet heavy-duty truck. The "Auto Service Co." may have drummed up some business for itself with this wreck.

A 1968 AMC Rambler 550 station wagon needs little more than a Band-Aid to repair the bent fender. A woman on her way to card club told the reporting officer that she "became nervous when she saw so many children running around that she got confused and stepped on the gas instead of the brakes, then slammed on the brakes and hit the house."

A 1969 Ford Mustang Mach I was demolished in what proved to be a deadly accident. After arguing with his girlfriend, the young motorist jumped behind the wheel and sped away. Broken hearts and broken lives lay among the shattered remains of a once beautiful machine.

A 1969 Chevrolet Camaro connected with a 1967 Chevrolet Bel Air four-door sedan. From the looks of things, the Bel Air driver backed out of the driveway in front of the oncoming Camaro.

A 1969 Chrysler and a 1973 Chevrolet Vega station wagon bottlenecked the highway along with crippling one another when they exchanged paint on a wet mountainside road. Note the dress-up, "groovy" paint job on the Vega.

This 1969 Chevrolet Impala two-door hardtop coupe with a 327 V-8 certainly has attracted the attention of the state police, who have clustered at the rear of the car. After skidding across the highway, the Chevy came to rest on its frame.

A 1969 Ford Mustang Mach I coupe, a road warrior's machine, could not keep it together on a backroad straightaway. The driver lost control and the rear came around and thumped a tree before the car crossed over the road to land in the underbrush. The police arrived in a 1970 Plymouth Fury police cruiser.

A 1969 Ford Fairlane four-door sedan is crumpled and shopworn from an encounter with an oncoming truck.

The family riding in this 1969 Oldsmobile Cutlass four-door sedan had an unpleasant ending to their vacation. No one was hurt when the travel trailer and car flipped and skated across the highway, coming to a standstill only after digging into the soft field. The National Guard heavy wrecker was called to remove both camper and car.

A 1969 Chevrolet Impala four-door hardtop had its pride destroyed by a big 1969 Cadillac DeVille four-door hardtop.

A 1969 Cadillac Coupe DeVille hardtop gets a disgusted look from the female driver of the 1967 Plymouth it chose to bump up against.

1970s

The decade started rather badly with escalations in Vietnam, the Kent State University tragedy, and Charles Manson. The Beatles split up. Jimmy Hendrix died of a drug overdose. Three Mile Island caused some excitement, as did an apartment complex in Washington called Watergate. John Wayne and Elvis checked out and the Arab Nations raised oil prices by 387 percent.

A headline in *The Washington Post* articulated America's anxieties: "Things Will Get Worse Before They Get Worse" The shining optimism of the '50s and early '60s had sadly waned. The mighty industrial engine of the previous two decades had stalled.

Legislation demanded that all new cars must be able to run on unleaded fuel. Safety regulations like side marker lights, seat belts, shoulder harnesses, rear window defoggers, dual circuit breakers, back-up lights, impact-absorbing interiors and windshield washers hit Detroit hard. The demands continued with the Clean Air Act, 5-mph impact bumpers, and mandatory emission regulations that forced manufacturers to detune engines. With an average American car getting about 13.5 miles per gallon, many of the laws were long overdue. The national speed limit was 55 mph. GM introduced airbags to a less than enthusiastic public.

The federal government also abolished the 7 percent excise tax on cars and imposed a 10 percent surcharge on all imports. And riding the wave of the legendary Beetle, VW became the first foreign manufacturer since 1930 to build cars in the U.S.

A 1970 Dodge Dart Swinger hardtop with a 383 Magnum V-8 cruised its way to annihilation. The clean engine compartment hints that this is a fairly new car.

A 1970 AMC Ambassador sedan sits alongside a much older Buick. Neither car is in very good shape.

A 1970 Ford LTD sedan lost traction as it proceeded down a dirt road, hammered a newly placed utility pole, slid around and thumped the back end into a sloped yard.

A 1970 Chevrolet Impala with a 350 engine left the dirt road and knocked plenty of bark off the trunk of a tree. Note the 1970 Plymouth Fury police car in the background.

A 1970 Ford Maverick took an ill-advised detour into a field. By the looks of the putty around the wheel well, someone was in the process of fixing up the old Maverick.

A 1970 Pontiac Grand Prix model J coupe and a 1971 Dodge Coronet four-door provide a little commotion for the residents.

A hot 1971 Dodge Charger should have found a more appropriate way to stop. Note the traction bars extending from the rear wheels. They didn't do much good in this case.

A 1971 Ford Pinto coupe was the means of transportation for a young girl going to the store to pick up rock salt to melt the ice on her sidewalks. She forgot that the roads would be icy too.

A passenger manages a smile while talking with an officer after a run-in involving a 1971 Chevrolet Chevelle Malibu four-door hardtop and a 1971 Chevrolet Monte Carlo two-door hardtop coupe.

A 1972 Chevrolet Monte Carlo two-door hardtop coupe wound up with the guts of its engine strewn about the ditch after an ugly highway mishap.

This 1972 Ford Gran Torino Sport hardtop coupe offered no luck for the Irish when, on St. Patrick's day, the driver went off the road and wrapped around a telephone pole on his way to a parade.

A 1973 Lincoln Continental two-door hardtop unintentionally broke into a store late one night. A crumpled fender and a shattered window are the extent of the damages from this fiasco.

A 1973 Mercury Cougar hardtop coupe was crunched beneath a trailer after being abandoned along a busy highway. The truck driver lost control when he hit the brakes in an attempt to avoid hitting the Cougar. The quick stop caused the trailer to shift loads and tip, right on top of the very vehicle he was trying so hard to avoid.

A 1973 Chevrolet Caprice Classic was all torn up after this incident.

Photo courtesy of *The Lock Haven Express*

A 1973 Plymouth Duster 340 two-door hardtop should be shown with a sign that reads "This Could Happen To You" to every driver that wants to scorch the highways. Accelerating to a very high rate of speed, the Duster crashed into and through several guardrails and a utility pole before nose-diving into a 200-foot ravine.

Photo courtesy of *The Lock Haven Express*

A 1974 Chevrolet Caprice gave a 1980 Oldsmobile Cutlass a messy piggyback ride.

A 1974 Plymouth Valiant got the worst of a collision with a 1973 Pontiac GTO with a 455-cid V-8 engine. A thin coating of ice was blamed for this accident.

A 1977 Mercury Monarch coupe was completely ravaged when it was struck and thrown into a snow-covered field by a freight train.

This 1978 Chevrolet Malibu Classic collided with a Ford Ranger pick-up truck and wound up on the sidewalk.

The driver of this 1978 Pontiac Bonneville needed medical attention after running his vehicle into a well-grounded restraining post. The post had been placed at the edge of the road the very afternoon of this accident. The property owner, having landscaped and seeded his yard many times after cars ripped through his lawn, took matters into his own hands and put up the post.

A big 1979 Mercury Marquis four-door sedan and its driver both took a bruising after this front-end hit.

Volkswagen

The two Volkswagens that were imported into United States in 1949 gave little evidence of the import revolution or the counter cultural icon the VW was to become by the 1960s. The "Peoples Car," commissioned by Adolph Hitler and designed by Ferdinand Porsche, found commercial success despite, or perhaps because of, its deviation from the basic design concepts set down by Henry Ford a half century earlier. The lightweight, air-cooled, rear-mounted, flat-four engine eliminated the need for a long drive shaft. The horizontally opposed cylinder configuration allowed for a short crankshaft and a fine fit with a proposed rear transaxle. Instead of a separate body and frame, the VW had a platform-type chassis with a central backbone and integral floor plan. Torsion bars were the choice for the front suspension and swing axles for the rear.

The intrinsic character and style remained virtually unchanged for the nearly three decades. During that time, the VW became one of the most remarkable phenomena in automobile history. Although improvements were made on a regular basis, Volkswagen paid little attention to model years.

The earliest Beetle, a nickname (along with "Bug" and "Puddle Jumper") used by American drivers, but never by the company, came equipped with 24-hp flat-four engine, which grew to 30 hp by 1949. The unsynchronized four-speed meant plenty of double clutching, while next to the gearshift was the manual choke button. Split windows, running boards and chrome-dome hubcaps are all familiar characteristics. The convertible was introduced in 1949; synchronized gearbox in 1952; larger and more rectangle back window late in 1958; turn signals were mounted atop the fender in 1959; padded sun visors replaced transparent plastic and an anti-sway bar was added in 1960; automatic choke, interior passenger grab handles and horizontal key slots came in 1961; and the gas gauge arrived in 1962.

By all indications 1976 was the final year the Volkswagen sedan was imported, but the demand for the new redesigned Beetle, which came out for 1998, stands as testimony to the love affair the public has had with this automobile superstar.

An inverted Beetle provided an exciting ride for someone. Note the jacket hanging from the bumper.

This VW was stopped in its tracks from the damages received on the back left fender.

This VW no longer qualifies as a "Great Masterpiece."

An unlucky VW had the squeeze put to it and required sheet metal on both sides of the front.

Is the police officer really telling the VW to "Stop right where you are!" If so, he should have given the order a bit sooner.

This poor little bug appears toothless without its bumper.

A Cadillac, sitting across the road, bullied this poor VW.

Photo courtesy of *The Williamsport Sun Gazette*

This shined, polished, and pinstriped VW probably was enjoying "Happy Motoring" prior to this mishap.

The driver's side door definitely doesn't close properly after this VW took a lick.

This little Bug created its own puddle to jump over by hitting a fire hydrant.

This VW wound up between a Renault Dauphine and a tree.

A badly damaged Volkswagen.